GERDA STEVENSON is an award-winn[
director and singer-songwriter. She l
television, radio, film and in opera,
abroad, and is a recipient of Scottish Arts Council and
Creative Scotland writers' bursaries. Her stage play, *Federer
Versus Murray*, directed by the author, toured to New York
in 2012 and was published there by Salmagundi. In 2014,
she was nominated as Scots Singer of the Year for the MG
Alba Scots Trad Music Awards, following the launch of
an album of her own songs, *Night Touches Day*. She has
written extensively for radio, including original plays and
dramatisations of Scottish novels. Her poetry collections,
If This Were Real (Smokestack Books, 2013), and *Quines:
Poems in Tribute to Women of Scotland* (Luath Press, first
edition 2018, second edition 2020), have been published
in Rome by Edizioni Ensemble in Italian translations by
Laura Maniero, 2017 and 2021, respectively. She wrote
the biographical introduction and a series of poems for the
book *Inside & Out: The Art of Christian Small* (Scotland
Street Press, 2019). She collaborated with Scottish landscape
photographer Allan Wright on their book *Edinburgh*, for
which she wrote the introduction and a sequence of 22 poems
(Allan Wright Photographic, 2019). In 2021, she directed a
film of George Mackay Brown's play *The Storm Watchers*, for
the St Magnus International Festival. A seasoned performer,
she won a BAFTA Best Film Actress award for her role in
Margaret Tait's feature film *Blue Black Permanent*, and is the
founder of Stellar Quines, Scotland's leading women's theatre
company. Her acclaimed book of short stories, *Letting Go: a
timeline of tales*, was published by Luath Press in 2021.

By the same author:

Prose
Letting Go: a timeline of tales (Luath Press, 2021)

Poetry
Quines: Poems in Tribute to Women of Scotland (Luath Press, first edition 2018, second edition 2020)
Quines: tributo poetico a donne della Scozia (Edizioni Ensemble, Rome, 2021)
Edinburgh (Allan Wright Photographic, 2019)
Inside & Out: The Art of Christian Small, with a biographical introduction and poems by Gerda Stevenson (Lyne Press, 2018; Scotland Street Press, 2019)
Se Questo Fosse Vero/If This Were Real (Edizioni Ensemble, Rome, 2017)
If This Were Real (Smokestack Books, 2013)

Plays for stage
Federer Versus Murray (Salmagundi, USA, 2012)
Pentlands At War, a community play, co-written with the Pentlands Writers' Group (Scottish Borders Council Library Services, 2006)

Plays for BBC radio
Room for Refugees (2017)
A Day Off (2015)
Homeless (2013)
Secrets (2011)
The Apple Tree (2011)
Island Blue, co-written with Iain Finlay MacLeod (2007)

For children
The Candlemaker and Other Stories, illustrated by the author (Kahn & Averill, 1987)

Tomorrow's Feast

GERDA STEVENSON

Luath Press Limited

EDINBURGH

www.luath.co.uk

First published 2023

ISBN: 978-1-80425-088-4

The paper used in this book is recyclable. It is made from low-chlorine
pulps produced in a low-energy, low-emission manner from
renewable forests.

Printed and bound by
Robertson Printers, Forfar

Typeset in 11 point Sabon LT by
Main Point Books, Edinburgh

Contents ·

Foreword by Meg Bateman   9

Prologue
Albatross   13

Heartwood
My Daughter's Painting   18
Orquil Burn   19
The Orkney Hood   21
Red Gloves in Kazimierz Dolny, Poland   22
Boy on a Bike   23
Old Photograph of a Young Woman   24
Traces   25
Decorating the Tree   26
Late Night Christmas Shopping   27
Cat-like   28
Lavender   29
My Mother-in-law's House   30

Corona
Lockdown   34
Hands   35
Covid-19 Reveals All   36
Biggin a Snaw Quine in Lockdoon   37
Dandelion Clock Haiku   38
Spiked Planet Haiku   39

Migrant Warker 40

Lockdown – Buchanan Street, Glasgow 41

Care Hame 42

Waving 44

Collective Breath

Little Boy 46

Mixed Messages 48

Hame-comin 49

Assad's Asset 50

The Baker of Idlib 51

The Alphabet of Jasmine 52

Fremmit 53

Russian Gloves 54

At the Astronomical Clock, Prague 55

I am the Airt 56

Atween Shooers/Between Showers 58

Bought and Sold

Song of the Slabhraidh 60

The Remembrancer 64

Newhaven 66

Til Ungdommen/Tae Youth 69

Mariner 71

Scots Glossary 105

Acknowledgements 111

For all the young ones
at tomorrow's feast

Foreword

Tomorrow's Feast is a collection of striking compassion. Stevenson's previous collection, *Quines*, had a particular agenda in celebrating the women of Scotland; this collection by contrast shows what moves her to poetry in her own times. While recognising our place in the 'terrible chain' of atrocities enacted on humanity and nature, *Tomorrow's Feast*, as the title implies, is entirely life-affirming, finding grace in the most extreme situations.

Three sections, with titles taken from lines in the poems, show a wide range of themes. *Heartwood* examines roots, parents and nurturing; *Corona*, sometimes serious and sometimes humorous (*Covid-19 Reveals All*), looks at the whole phenomenon of lockdown with glimpses of nature and our reassessment of our values. The poems in *Collective Breath* expose the toxic mix of capitalism and Christianity (*Little Boy*), and the greed and destruction of war.

Of equal importance to *what* a poet writes is *how* a poet writes about it. Stevenson uses a range of different voices (always pitch-perfect), often revealing a vulnerability and humanity we don't see from our usual perspectives. She speaks as a burn, or the North Esk Reservoir, as a woman in Iron Age Orkney or in a care-home during lockdown, as a soldier who has seen too much. Her voice in Scots brings out the utmost lyricism in poems like 'Fremmit' and 'Hame-comin'. Her poems are in the moment; in the 'prism where the light is refracted'. A tight weaving of scenes lets images take on symbolic weight. There is also a delight in words, and a streak of black humour.

The collection ends with the libretto *Mariner* based on

Coleridge's *The Rime of the Ancient Mariner*. It held me spellbound in the way it echoes that great poem in narrative, rhythm and vocabulary, while giving it a new reading as a plea for justice, for humanity and nature in the face of our current refugee and ecological crisis. It is a *tour de force*, expanding the main themes of the collection, and demonstrating Stevenson's great powers of imagination, narrative and fun.

Meg Bateman,
February 2023

Prologue

Albatross

in mind of 'The Rime of the Ancient Mariner,'
by Samuel Taylor Coleridge

Not the first, that mariner,
and not the last, to kill my kind,
take aim and break the arc
of free-wheeling flight,
still the heart
in mid-air.

Perhaps he feared the power
of ghostly cargo – some say
we carry the souls of drowned mariners;
if so, they never weighed me down:
my wingspan – twice my killer's height –
featherlight in windward climb,
leeward descent to spindrift,
reverse turn above cresting waves
into the flow of ascent again
till his arrow
hit home.

Or maybe it was envy –
I could tack the wind
as well as any sailboat, fly
the earth's girth without landfall
in less than two full moons
and make it back
to the same nest.

Did it cross his mind as he lifted his bow
that my life-long mate might be waiting there,
warming our egg, that bright oval, heartbeats
syncopating through feathers and shell,
my turn to forage? We'd taken time
to choose each other, he and I,
an earth-bound dance of many moves,
rising on web foot tip-toe,
wings not locked for flight,
but held out wide in a perfect curve
for land-based balance, beaks
trumpeting our union straight up
to the sky.

I followed the ship for men's scraps,
learned the tune of the mariner's call
as he waved to me, my nourisher;
and for good measure,
displayed my manoeuvres
in breeze and squall,
looped and soared, all
for his pleasure.

Why did my mariner turn on me?
Was it sudden anger at the knack
we planet wanderers have
of drinking ocean water,
and him dreading his ship's store
from rain and rivers
might be running dry?

Or was it terror of a wild mystery
in all I could do that overwhelmed
him and – when I fell – his crew,
who couldn't gauge if his act
should be condemned
or praised?

I was no threat, no burden,
no curse. I was just there,
riding the air.

Heartwood

My Daughter's Painting

What was it you saw
with your unseen
third eye and invisible
extra chromosome,
as you put paint to paper?
Was it a tree, with its trunk
and crown, or
did you see yourself,
a young woman reaching
from the heartwood,
feeling your tap root
anchored to earth,
your bark a gown
of folded colours wrapped
around those hidden inner rings,
each one bright as Saturn's,
as you stretched your branched arms
into the stars, shaking the deep
blue night of the cosmos
to shower our forlorn planet
with leaves of light,
that we might
see it as you do –
the first garden, where
all was new and equal,
and knowledge good?

Orquil Burn
after a film by Margaret Tait

I rise in a quiet place, tranquil, like my name,
where the lone owl swoops above constellations
of bog cotton and sphagnum moss; water drips
from roots, and I trickle by gravity's instinct,
meander through abandoned peat banks
to curlew's call, past orchids and butterwort,
no thought of my own utility;

till I'm commandeered –
diverted to power a mill,
a handy back-up plan
when the wind blows herself out,
and for a while Orkney lies still.
I'm bridged, dammed and fenced –
barbed wire marks men's borders;
even my name is implicated:
'liquor' lurks in its letters
as I'm piped to the distillery.
I learn to flow the man-made way
in straight lines, by Caldale Camp,
its concrete wartime hearths
bereft of walls in desolate ranks,
declaring dereliction to the sky;

but flowers still come to soften my banks,
yellow mimulus and meadowsweet,
and boys gather round me to play
in the 'deep places', they say, deft fingers
weaving iris-leaf boats – green vessels gliding slow,
stalking each other to childish cries of 'Torpedo!' –
echo of battles a stone's throw from my estuary,
where I plunge over rocks into the tidal to and fro,
and mingle among history's wreckage
in salty Scapa Flow.

The Orkney Hood

an Iron Age child's garment, now in the National Museum of Scotland, discovered perfectly intact, buried in a peat bog at Groatsetter, Orkney

Like the good hunter he is,
your father brought the trophy home –
not meat, but this fringed band
of woven moorit wool, washed up
on the shore, tangled in seaweed,
the weave of it styled
to adorn the highest born.

Second hand, I'll make it new for you,
my peedie bairn (though I'm no stitcher
to a chieftain's court), enough in its length
to grace the hem of a hood I'll cut
from the good part of mother's old shawl;
her herringbone weave will hug
your blessèd head, shield you
from chill wind, and when you dance,
the fine fringe will fly at your shoulders
like the sun's rays.

Red Gloves in Kazimierz Dolny, Poland

You chose red gloves,
work of a proud old lace-maker,
who didn't soften in the face
of your extra chromosome, but stuck
to her price in the market place
of the town named for a great king.

You wore them with all the grace
of his belovèd Esterka, offering a poised
hand to the dapper gypsy man
who serenaded you: 'Little girl
of bright colours, the world
is open for you,' he improvised
with his scarred guitar and broken smile;

and as we crossed the majestic Vistula,
you waved the colour of your pleasure to the world.

Boy on a Bike

Crunch of rubber on grit
and I wake from a car park doze
to you – a spark in my windscreen –
blue jacket, hair aflame, its fire
a challenge to bare trees
that straggle their geometry
around this forgotten suburb.

Disco beats from the bowling club,
a hammer clatters in someone's yard;
the year dwindles to another grey sleep
as you stream on spinning wheels,
out of sight and into your life.

Old Photograph of a Young Woman

in memoriam Marilyn Imrie, 1947–2020

I didn't know you then,
wind-blown lass, happed
in your winter coat –
time was all ahead,
like the kite you guide
on a single gossamer thread
and only you can see,
its flight path beyond the frame;

everything is light
in this faded black and white –
your skin, your smile, the sky,
the bright sand of a Fife shore,
your future flying before.

Traces

Yesterday we walked after snowfall
as the North Star rose; and today,
minus five snaring my breath
on the morning air, I find our mark
still there, the print of your small boots
set in ice, and next to them, mine,
their measured partner, all the way.
I place my feet in old tracks,
while you're elsewhere making new ones –
the ploughs were out as we slept,
and the school bus made it through.

I hug our journeys these days,
try to hold them, crystallised,
as you stride from them,
all traces melted in your eager mind
like the thaw that's to come.

Decorating the Tree

Here they come again
in the darkest time,
carried into light
from their attic hibernation,
a mute congregation, loud
with memories – so many now
some have begun to fade –
a robin of lost origin, its frayed breast
still a red song on a green branch,
and a finless fish whose sequined eye
in recent years has caught mine
with 'Where?' and 'Why?'

But not these two clay stars
you gave me, terracotta, unglazed,
the down-to-earth grain of you
warm in my palms, yet
the stab of your absence
as I fold my fingers over
each pentagram, their points
pricking my skin, pressing home
the hard fact that you are unreachable
stardust now.

Late Night Christmas Shopping

'Anything last minute you still need?'
I ask my mother, well aware that need
can't be in it; and, to avoid the crowds,
delay till the eleventh hour, then drive
through sleet beneath a racing moon –
swoop of owl past my windscreen –
five miles to the nearest town,
where Tesco stamps itself red on the night.

'What time do you close?'
I ask a lonely shelf-stacker
down a deserted aisle. 'We don't,'
he laments, 'God knows why –
hardly anyone's buying, and I'm on till 7.'
But he musters a smile in fluorescent glare,
directing me to pickled walnuts and marzipan.

I'm relieved to find such things are there,
in spite of hunger and carnage
under the same moon, and my place
in their terrible chain;
glad that my mother's hands,
after long years of sustaining us all,
will place on her table, once again,
her annual offerings at tomorrow's feast.

Cat-like

'You're like a cat,' my mother told me
when I was young, 'you make yourself better.'
But in that secret, cat-like way,
I'd always wondered how that day
would feel when at last it came.
Would I be like a cat *then*?

I like cats, but as the day drew near,
I grew doubtful, sensed a wild one
might be stalking by your bed. I sang songs,
made sure the prowler wouldn't pounce
on my watch, asked for the smile you gave
with sweet grace, an ancient child
in its lop-sided curve, though in your eyes
I glimpsed an unknown place –
a slow, dark river, and a shadow moving
on the far bank by a gleam
of stepping stones.

That day was only yesterday; it crept in
with dawn, like cats do, on silent paws,
seizing the chance. Now it's passed,
and in a shop window a cat yawns
from a patch of sunlight. Our eyes meet.
It blinks, then nestles into itself.
I walk on.

Lavender

We chose lavender,
to be carried with your coffin,
your favourite, native
to the Old World,
like the essence of you,
lavandula – holy to the Romans,
prized by the Greeks for its power
to lead the way to sleep;
dried stems, it had to be,
for your last journey, Spring
too early for new blooms,
the bouquet cradled
by my daughter in your wake
to the slow farewell of *The Queen's Dolour*,
intense the scent as she passed our row,
each bud brushing the air –
invisible clouds drifting, rising
on every note,
lavender, lavandula,
farewell father, *lavender,*
lavender, lavandula.

Note: lavandula is the Latin name for lavender; the stress comes on the
second vowel, lavandula.

My Mother-in-law's House

Twice I went back after she left
for that other world, the kingdom
she prayed might let her in
through its troubling doorway,
narrower than a needle's eye;
she'd lived a simple life, after all,
a frugal widow, lowly and prayerful,
had done her best to qualify for admittance,
though she knew her son would be barred
the moment he told her he didn't believe.

Twice I went back – had to crouch down
the first time to enter the rusted gate,
beneath untamed escallonia that claimed
the garden wall; doors locked, front
and back, whitewash weeping
stains of neglect, windowpanes veiled
by storm-driven salt from the Minch.
I licked my palms to clear spy-holes
into empty rooms, watched
invisible gatherings – Gaelic chat
over a *strùpag,* her featherlight pancakes
laden with crowdie, fresh from her own cow;
heard psalms spiral the sealed silence,
sung by elders around the hearth
in those nights between death
and burial, before her will was read.

Twice I went back – the second time
another world: trimmed and fenced,
extended walls gleaming white
behind a battery of cars, all gated
by the owners – new voices
from the Midlands in the Northern air,
terms stated: Private Driveway.
No Stopping or Turning. Keep Out.

Corona

Lockdown

The wind picks up – a blue-green surge
among the firs, as I walk the forest circle,
my single outdoor ration for the day.
Cone coronas wave on boughs above,
the fallen ones crackling at my heels,
seeding their next generation.
I lean into a tree root and breathe deep
the green tincture of sphagnum's antiseptic stars,
imagine I'm inhaling a vaccine,
elusive elixir that will shield me
when I run the gauntlet for vulnerable loved ones
between supermarket shelves.

The wind lulls – somewhere in the pines'
fathomless layers cooshie-doos croon
and flutter their muffled wings;
far off, the whine of light aircraft –
the infected prince, perhaps, on his way
to that handy fallback of Highland isolation.

Hands

to all our NHS staff and care workers

Two minutes to eight. We wrap up,
step out and wait; no moon or stars to light
this lampless pinpoint on the planet's map –
night hushed, happed in mist.
Across the field, behind the hill,
invisible hands are poised;
we listen, uncertain who will lead:
out there, through the dark,
the first palms give their little strike,
and we offer ours; more follow,
ghostly applause tapping the damp air –
flesh we've washed and washed, rough
with trying to keep the killer at bay –
neighbours giving thanks
to all those anonymous hands
holding onto life for us.

Covid-19 Reveals All

'Out of stock everywhere,' she said.
'Only six weeks till we know
everyone's true hair colour.'
I stopped dead –
vanity rearing its ugly head:
I'll look like a badger in no time,
or a mad magpie flitting out and in
when the fishman calls; the stark line
between dark and light at my parting,
marking the start of Lockdown.
The difference a dearth of hair dye makes
is clear as day and night – I'll be a fright!
Why did I not have the foresight,
the downright faith in my feminist roots,
those hard-earned, seasoned attributes,
to let nature take its course, go back
(in carefully shaded, coiffured stages)
to the source? Too late. As the dreaded grey
progresses, gone the chance
to be a goddess of silver tresses.
It's that time: old bat time.
Or hat time.

Biggin a Snaw Quine in Lockdoon

Nae need fur insistence
on social distance:
ye're safe, ye're fine,
wi a benign snaw quine.

Dandelion Clock Haiku

Snow-white corona
releasing seeds on wind's breath
to grow into gold.

Spiked Planet Haiku

Manhattan, Hong Kong:
coated concrete columns gleam
like Covid-19.

Migrant Warker

on reading Arundhati Roy's essay, 'The Pandemic is a Portal'

It cam sae suddent, the lockdoon –
guns jabbin oor backs, aawhaur baured,
naewhaur tae bide.
We were in the swatshoap,
ma bairns an me, at the machines,
stitchin zips, three hunner atween us an oor,
pirn-threid castin stour
throu a gash o licht blearin ma veesion;
sae blin I wis, an distractit bi the gairds' clatter
at the stairheid, I near tint ma fingers
in the needle's dreel.
'Hame wi yez!' they skraikit, 'Hame!'
But whaur's thon? We cam here
years syne, scrappin fur wark,
an hae grindit oor darg sae lang,
it's aa we ken – there's nae gangin back.
I climp a swatch o claith
tae mak a bield for us come nicht,
cramasie gaberdine, gear fur a queen,
bag it unner ma sark, an we're oot –
shoothers, hurdies, breists
dunchin intae fowk like hirdit coos
in muckle swaws as faur's oor een can see;
ma bairns grup at me an greet,
but nae comfort can I gie;
yon claith I reived wull mairlike be
oor windin sheet nor bield,
for we hae been forsaken shairly:
a braithin chain, ilk link growthie grun
fur the sleekit canker tae spreid its hornit croon.

Lockdown – Buchanan Street, Glasgow

I saw a young roe deer today,
not here among hills
where there's no surprise
in their easy presence, but online –
hand-held footage caught
on an empty concourse: antlers
branching between steel bollards
and abandoned shop fronts, hooves
tapping concrete in a leggy dash
through no man's land for safe ground;

had it broken from the herd
like a teenage rebel intent
on striking out alone, or
did an old knowledge flood
its senses with the morning sun
drawing it into the city's coma
to seek the once green hollow?

Note: the name Glasgow derives from the Brythonic (Welsh) 'glas-cau',
meaning 'green hollow'.

Care Hame

Aawhaur here is white,
sae cauld an white. No like snaw,
thir fower waas that haud me ticht
an steekit in, nor cloods neethur –
I'd no mind *yon*, snell braith
o the lift in baith – but naw,
naethin saft aboot them,
juist the haurd white o nae life.
I gove sae lang at ae space –
whit else tae dae? –
I'm seein the white o ma ain een.

Whiles a wumman comes ben –
the same yin? Could be twa, three,
I dinnae ken, mibbe mair, a hale team –
happit in plastic, white gloves, an maskit
like astronauts; they gie me white pills
wheemer at me wi white wurds;
the lest yin gied a white lauch
like crackit ice ahint the mask
whan I askit 'Whit's the score?'
'Weel,' she says, 'we're no winnin yet,
but we'll get there,' an wuns awa,
me wunnerin whaur, *whaur*
wull we get tae? An when?

Wull it still be white, thon place,
or reid, like the bluid-brainches
ablow ma lids when I steek ma een
agin the knife o the ceilin licht
an dwaum o green birks up the brae at hame?
Or wull it be gowd, the gowd o yon lauch –
I mind it wis ma dochter's –
afore the warld turnt white?

Waving

Years now, since the solemn men
from the Co-op came, and zipped you
into a blue bag. Not your style.
I took your black fedora
from its hook in the hall and donned it
for you on the doorstep, waving,
as they drove you off into the void.

Today you're waving in my laptop screen
from your garden cabin window,
wearing your Chinese mandarin hat,
laughter muted by the pane of glass,
your small granddaughter waving back
above ruby tulips, hands held high
in the late Spring light.

This child of mine, almost an adult now,
looks over my shoulder,
considers the snapshot,
and, solemn as those men, says:
'We were Social Distancing then,
Grandad and me' – as if the virus,
not content with claiming the present,
has colonised our past.

Collective Breath

Little Boy

Little Boy is on his way, snug
in the metal womb of *Enola Gay*,
all of his components prepped,
but not quite ready yet –
his system fine-tuned only after take-off –
safety first for his birthing crew.
The pilot gives full throttle:
'Do it for me, Momma!'
Overloaded, *Enola Gay*
eats up the whole runway –
'Momma, come ON!' –
and lifts into night;

six hours to go;
lieutenant and weaponeer
grope in torchlight
along the portside catwalk
to the pitch-black bay,
armed with Thy might
in the name of Jesus Christ –
the chaplain's prayer before flight
that nailed their mission to the cross
and gave it a tail wind of righteousness;

and he's primed now – no going back –
Little Boy, nestling there,
like the baby saviour
in the virgin's amniotic sac,
carried into that bright morning
on the last, steep climb
to bombing altitude,
and then

let go;
falling,
six miles
in 44 seconds,
falling
to Hiroshima below,
where someone called Kazuko
lifts her child from his cot,
the River Ota outside, its seven streams
full and tranquil – slack water at high tide,
while far above in cloud-flecked blue
Enola Gay banks into her getaway –
a nine-mile dash – and makes it
by a hair's breadth, chased by shimmers
from a ghostly flash;

barely born, *Little Boy* has made his mark:
lit ten thousand suns at every window,
then snuffed them out, shocked eyeballs
from sockets into palms, skin to rags –
futile surrender flags in sudden twilit limbo –
lungs and throats a desert drought,
bodies burning at four thousand celsius
from the inside out.

Note: *Little Boy* was the codename for the atomic bomb dropped on the
Japanese city of Hiroshima on 6 August 1945, the first nuclear weapon
used in warfare. *Little Boy* was dropped by the Boeing B-29 Superfortress
Enola Gay, named after Enola Gay Tibbets, the mother of the pilot, Colonel
Paul Tibbets. The accompanying observation planes were named *The Great
Artiste* and *Necessary Evil*.

Mixed Messages

He was biding in London at the time, all the way
from the Pentland Hills, where he'd grown up –
never a thought of police and bombs
among drystane dykes, the nine Scots pines
at Crooked Jock on the ridge above the burn
marching like giants at his shoulder as he'd skip
down the brae to the shop for his Ma, to get
messages – milk, bread and pork links, and whiles
a sweetie, if she'd a shine on her face that day.

And now he was in The Big Smoke, houseboy
for a lady whose Chelsea bedroom was filled
with potted hyacinths – one of his jobs to water them,
a heady-scented azure haze that made him dwaum.
He liked to sneak in when she was out,
imagine himself as Tam Lin the Elfin Knight,
locked in the charmed glen,
waiting for Fair Janet to break the spell.

Sirens were yammering that day, time of the IRA,
blue lights flashing, folk in a stooshie
to get out the road and home, when a bobby
lands a hand on his shoulder, thwak!
'Where you going, mate?' 'B-b-back to the flat,'
he habbers, feeling, for no reason he can nail,
like a right glaikit, guilty sumph.
'And what's in your bag?'
'Messages,' he says, the innocent items dunt-
dunting his shoogling knees. 'Just messages.'

And that was it – milk, bread and a string of links
nabbed; and him locked up for a night in the clink.

Hame-comin

a sodjer returns frae Afghanistan

Hame, hame, hame on the truck,
the wheels grind their grumly air,
hame tae ma mither, ma faither, ma lass,
but I canna come hame in ma hert nae mair,
noo that ma freends are laid in the grund,
and the desert sun has blurred ma een,
stoor in ma mind frae yon cramasie flooer
that smoors aa pain on field and street,
no, I canna, canna come hame in ma hert
noo I've duin whit I've duin
(orders are orders, ye dae whit ye maun),
and I've seen whit I've seen:

oh, the bluid that brak through her skin
like a flooer frae its bud, yon bairn
that cam runnin, birlin, lauchin, skirlin
intae the faimily dance o mirth
we blew tae hell like a smirr o eldritch confetti;

and noo I'm here, hame on the truck,
ma freends in the grund, but I canna come hame
nae mair in ma hert, for hame's naewhaur
when yer hert's deid – nae langer sair – juist deid
wi dule and the wecht o bluid fallin like flooers,
cramasie flooers, that kill aa pain, smoor yer mind,
deid, deid, as the wheels grind.

Assad's Asset

She mingles with him at the Vatican
among the world's mighty men.
A London banker, schooled
in England's green and private shires,
she looks no more than a slip-of-a-girl,
wife to the one-time eye doctor
whose baby-blue iris pools belie the tale
of means and ends their pupils nail.
Cameras click on her ready smile
as it glides like a lovely summer boat
through perfumed waves of barbered
and absurdly hatted heads, her dagger-heeled tread
light and sure-footed on Rome's holy ground;
who'd guess such trained finesse could lend itself
to murderous intrigue in vast marble halls,
and brazen slaughter on blasted streets?
She gives a sheen to proceedings –
finely tuned as an Arab horse,
perfect pedigree to secure the dynastic line.

The Baker of Idlib

His children didn't know yet
that in his shop he now lay dead,
cooling fingertips rimmed with flour.

Every morning as bombs fell
the aroma of hope had risen
with lightness from his palms,
white dough plied to pale softness,
and baked into crusted gold – loaves
he'd carry through the shattered street
to eager hands at broken thresholds,
his pledge to nourish life
at the edge of extremity,
bread like a blessing,
his blessing of bread.

The Alphabet of Jasmine

for Nizar Qabbani

'Damascus,' said the poet, 'was the womb
that gave me the alphabet of jasmine' –
his language, shaping fine thought
like petals etched in moonlight,
carrying the scent of love;
but now, when skies grow dark with hate,
and land is turned to dust,
the alphabet of jasmine withers on its stem,
blackened at the root below broken stone.
Will his people, in their exodus
still speak that glittering blend?
Will the seeds lie dormant till they return?
They are crossing a bitter sea with no words,
leaving the homeland that gave them
long ago the alphabet of jasmine.
Will it remember them? Will it grow green shoots
in their memory when the last drone leaves the sky
and a new-born infant's cry rises on the timid air?
Will the alphabet of jasmine bloom on that child's tongue
like the flowers a grandmother sets in the window
to welcome her family when they, at last, come home?

Fremmit

in memoriam Alan Kurdi

Nine faddoms deep they lie the nicht
faur frae the hame they ken,
davert tae the seals an shairks
that straik their strippit banes.
The ghaistly muin abuin them sails
in a black an wappin lift;
fur aa their licht the starns are blin,
thae bairns are tint for aye;
their kin micht sab, mithers scraich
their grief tae heiven's hicht –
the hale warld, ow'r aa its airts,
hus boardit up and nailed ticht
its hert's door fur fear o fremmit fowk,
their fremmit weys –
thae bairns are gane fur aye.

Wha wull say wha taks the wyte,
wha cairries shame in the auld gemm
o win or tyne? Sin lang syne men
hae seen their mercats rise an faa,
collateral the stamp o nature's law;
cauld blasts in Januar will bring
feast an sang: *Let us pray that come it may,*
brithers be, an aa that; aa that, fur aa that –
nine faddoms deep they lie the nicht;
thae fremmit bairns o fremmit fowk,
deid an gane fur aye.

Russian Gloves

I happened to be wearing them
that Sunday morning, news of Ukraine
bleeding from the radio as I left the house
to join neighbours at our local attraction –
the red coffee van, a new heart beat
drawing us together, a constant trickle
for an hour or so along the village arteries – life
after the virus opening up, the aroma
of freshly ground beans teasing our nostrils
in the frosted air;

and there, in the car park, our ankles fringed
by snowdrops – white lanterns expanding
in the sun – my gloves are admired
for their intricate pattern, Fair Isle style,
with a Tatar touch, egg-shell blue, green
and yellow, 'Spring colours to lift our spirits,'
someone says, and I remind her
of the Russian woman who lived for a while
over the hill, became my friend,
and made them for me, deft fingers
flicking wool between needles' click,
those supple, expert hands I know so well,
and often think of in everything they do;

and then a man says it – casts a tiny grenade
into the morning: 'So they'll be for the bin,
won't they!' and a small cloud of hatred hangs
in the soured air.

At the Astronomical Clock, Prague

Thunder clouds discharge a deluge
on Old Town Square, as if they've held
too long the memory of Noah's Flood;
cataracts teem from sodden scalps down
rat-tailed hair, between hustling umbrellas.

But who cares? We're here, alive,
and though we've as many sounds
in our mouths as Babel's Tower, right now
we're one, laughing at the skeleton,
who strikes each second to the deadline,
as the windows open and the Twelve Apostles
take the air in their hourly mechanical stroll.
We hold a collective breath,
willing the moment not to be over,
before the windows close –
the same frame held in little Kafka's eyes,
dragged across the square to school each day
by the hollow-cheeked, angry cook,
time ticking at his infant wits;

and it's passed, the skeleton at rest.
No let-up in the rain, as we drift apart
into another hour.

I Am the Airt

Life and Times of North Esk Reservoir

I am the airt fowk tramp in sairch o quate,
faur frae the toon's ding-dang in the lang, late
simmer oors, or in a blink o winter licht –
nae soond but the tirlin sang o whaup
on the wund's souch.

Tho seein me noo ye'd nivver ken
I wisnae aye sae douce – I hae owerseen
time's dirdum: I cairry merks o the warld's slaw birth
beddit in ma craigs and bields – the prent o Silurian fins
that flichtert aince 'mang muckle swaws –
thae braw faulds o saut watter whan I wis an ocean,
braid and deep.

Syne, at lest, the faem seeped awa tae kythe
ma green braes, risin frae a lochan smaa
whaur sea hud raired, and aawhaur,
insteid o fish, the yird's starns shawed –
gress o Parnassus, gowans, and mey spink;

till, ae day, athoot warnin, the blatter o hooves,
dunder o cairts, clatter o buits: hunners o men
howk, heeze and lig stanes, biggin ma watter intae a dam
tae pouer the Empire's mills; whae'd hae thocht! –
yowdendrifts o paper blawin oot tae the warld
fur prent – Scott's Waverley tales, aa the sangs o Burns,
and pent – the bleezin mists o Turner's veesions.

Lang syne the mills hae fauldit, mercats scauldit
in feckless fechts tae hae their gear bocht and sauld;
aince mair, ootthrou the year, I am the airt whaur quate
rings in the late simmer oors, or in a blink o winter licht;
nae soond the day, save a reeshle o braith on the loch's face
and a lanely whaup's tirlin sang on the wund's souch.

Note: 440 million years ago, the North Esk Reservoir was part of an ocean environment. Since the 19th century, for over a hundred years, the nearby town of Penicuik was one of the British Empire's largest paper producers. The water that powered its mills was regulated by the reservoir, high in the Pentland Hills.

Atween Shooers

Anely a glisk it took,
staunin there amang trees,
tae lat it aa gae;
needles o yallaein larik
lown in thair faa,
a gled line o bird caa
through quate fidder
o russet an gowd
lowsed frae birk an gean;
blue firs in fauld on fauld
o liftin mist, an syne, ance mair,
the douce hiss o siftin smirr.

Between Showers

Only a moment, it took,
standing there among trees,
to let it all go;
needles of yellowing larch
in noiseless fall,
a clear line of bird call
through mute flutter
of russet and gold
released from birch and gean;
blue firs in fold upon fold
of rising mist, and then
the gentle hiss
of sifting drizzle again.

Note: Neither poem is a translation of the other – both were somehow
written simultaneously.

58

Bought and Sold
sprechgesang – words to be spoken and sung

Song of the Slabhraidh

in tribute to Donald and Anne MacPherson who sailed on the emigrant ship, the Priscilla, *taking their slabhraidh with them, from the Isle of Skye to Melbourne; and to their Australian relatives, who still have the slabhraidh*

Chorus:
I am the slabhraidh, the hook and chain,
each link holds a story, the old refrain
of loss and profit, greed and gain,
of people and places, so many faces,
and too many farewells, again and again.

Greaulainn my birthplace, and my first home,
once a land of milk and honeycomb,
forged by the blacksmith to honour a debt
he owed to Donald, I'll never forget
the tap, tap, tap of hammer on anvil,
the sparks that flew as he coaxed through fire
my form, good and true; debt
branded into my iron soul,
from the outset, debt, and it takes its toll,
for debt is the net that rich men cast,
to trap the people of Greaulainn.

Chorus: I am the slabhraidh, the hook and chain, etc...

Hung from the rafters, I kept my place,
holding the pot above the hearth, ready, always,
for family grace, though ceilidhs were seldom,
for Anne's sunken face told of hunger,
and Donald's too, and their stick-thin wee bairn,
already snared by the blight of famine –
how could they last through another cold blast
of winter, here in Greaulainn? What could they do?

The bible won't feed you when rent is due,
and no way to pay it; till the mighty men of the mills
step in, the mighty mill-men of Yorkshire.
The wool trade's how their money's made –
wool into gold – like the tales I've heard told
in days of old round the peat fire;
bought and sold, for wool into gold,
the fate of the people from Greaulainn.

Chorus: I am the slabhraidh, the hook and chain, etc...

The mill-men's shepherds across the sea
had abandoned their flocks in Melbourne
in the frenzied flush, the headlong crush to the gold rush,
and profit's clock was slowing down, tick, tock, tick, tock,
'Those Island Jocks,' the mill-men said,
'need to pull themselves up by the bootstrap.
They'll plug the gap.' And word is out, it's in the air,
the word is out everywhere: *emigrate, emigrate* –
they have a date, and this is my fate:
packed in a blanket of woven tweed –
there will always be need of a slabhraidh
wherever their hearth, in whichever land,
for Donald and Anne from Greaulainn.

Chorus: I am the slabhraidh, the hook and chain, etc...

The *Priscilla* was docked, and the poor people flocked
to embark at the harbour in Liverpool,
from all over Skye, and St Kilda too,
three hundred souls, give or take a few –
from Uig, and Carbost, Sligachan, Teangue,
Romisdale, Bernisdale, Struan, Portree,
Herbusta, Skeabost, Bundalloch, Kilvaxter,

Camusunary, Camustianavaig, Ferrindonald and Glasphen,
Achnahannait, Hungladder, and my three among them –
Donald and Anne and the bairn...
and me, happed in tweed, from Greaulainn.

Chorus: I am the slabhraidh, the hook and chain, etc...

Priscilla sounds sweet, *Priscilla* sounds neat,
but hell, she was, hell, as the ocean heaved –
oh, who would believe my story?
Each dawn a death knell, as another life fell
to fever and plague – the bairn, our wee bairn,
you could build a cairn with the lives we gave
to the towering waves that took them down
to a deep salt grave; those long, long months
in that rolling hold, and all for gold, gold, gold,
but not for Donald, and not for Anne,
no gold for them or their lost wee bairns –
a second one born on the pitching sea,
now both lie dead on the cold ocean bed,
so far, so far from Greaulainn.

Chorus: I am the slabhraidh, the hook and chain, etc...

The world is wide and tribes are many,
but aye the poor are ten a penny,
like the starving souls of Greaulainn,
dispatched Down Under without a map,
to pull themselves up by the bootstrap,
tossed onto a parched plain,
where the sun beat down with no rain,
and nothing grew that they knew to eat –
only long, brittle grass – and the bleat, bleat
from herds of sheep in the bone-dry heat;

and all the while dark people watched
like ghosts behind rocks in their dreaming,
dark people silent and watching
the latest invaders scarring their land –
the weary folk from Greaulainn.

Chorus: I am the slabhraidh, the hook and chain, etc...

Years have passed since that long odyssey,
and Greaulainn, I'm told, is broken stone,
abandoned on the slopes above Linicro.
Many a rafter has borne my weight,
while I held the pot – the light freight
of thin broth, never the lot of Donald and Anne
to sit at the hearth to a banquet.
All their bairns died, bairn after bairn,
save one, who survived, and carried the line
down to this day, handing me on to tell the tale,
a witness to the world's way
and the fate of the people of Greaulainn.

Chorus:
Yes, I am the slabhraidh, the hook and chain,
each link holds a story, the old refrain
of loss and profit, greed and gain,
of people and places, so many faces,
and too many farewells, again and again.

Note: In September 1852, 298 inhabitants of St Kilda and the Isle of Skye
left for Australia on board the *Priscilla*. The ship was carrying starving,
poverty-stricken emigrants under a new scheme funded by the Highland and
Island Emigration Society. The death toll was 31 on board, and another 11
died at the quarantine station in Australia. The emigrants were subsequently
required to repay the Society the funds they had been granted so the sum
could be re-invested to facilitate further emigration.

The Remembrancer (or Noo We Ken)

in the style of Gilbert and Sullivan – sort of

I am the very model of a true British anachronism,
my title, wig and gown they reek of darkest medievalism,
Henry the Eighth set up my post to scotch egalitarianism,
I'm here to safeguard London's holy realm of ca-pi-tal-ism.

I'm unelected, I'm protected ('cause we have no constitution),
my remit: to promote all profit, lobby every institution
that can increase the City's power – my unique contribution:
I undermine and roadblock any equal distribution.

Remembrancer, Remembrancer, we didnae huv a clue till noo
of who you were, Sir, who you were! We didnae huv a scoobie-doo!

Sometimes you'll see me in the House of Commons, and the Lords as well,
I have unfettered access to whoever serves my clientele,
I'm quiet, I'm discreet, polite, I never leave a nasty smell,
an icon of the British state, magician of the Citadel.

My budget is a tidy sum – around 5 million per annum,
it's not for you, it's for the banks (and me) watch out – *Cave Canem!*
Hi-hip-hoorah, it's not for you – I'm serving glorious Mammon.
Cave Canem – beware the fangs of 5 million per annum.

We didnae huv a scoobie-doo that you were even there, Sir,
but noo we ken, we'll no forget: Remembrancer, Remembrancer.

It's always been a man's job, mine, without exception, every time:
Norton, Fletcher, Edmonds, Dearham, Burrowes, Lightfoot, Dalton, Hind.
It's like a club, our heart-beats rhyme with every stroke of Big Ben's chime,
I'm Mr Double, glad to share with you a glass of vintage wine.

Whit – Double, as in standards? Shairly no – it's too good! Mr Double!
As in Shakespeare's Scottish play – the witches stirrin up yon trouble?
Mr Double! How d'ye dae, fire burn and cauldron bubble,
ye couldnae mak it up, no sir, a Remembrancer called Mr Double!

I never should have spoken out, incognito I carry clout,
but prospects of another crash and lobbying to be bailed out
has got me fired up, all excited, keener than a young Boy Scout,
I'm salivating at the thought of a tasty leveraged buyout.

He's got himsel fired up, excited, keener than a wee Boy Scout,
he's gantin at the thocht o a muckle leveraged buyout!

We didnae huv a scoobie-doo but noo we dae, ye mak us spew!
Ye're juist a symptom o a system that's bankrupt – its time is due.
We're bailin oot, we're dumpin you, yer wig, yer flag, red, white an blue,
Remembrancer, 'bye bye' tae you, ta-ta tae you and aa yer crew!

They've rumbled me, they've tumbled to it, they really feel I make them spew,
they're bailing out, they're dumping me, my wig, my flag, red, white and blue.

You're frae anither planet, pal – ye might as weel hae come frae Mars!
Go stick yer banks, consultants, grey suits and yer Gherkin up yer arse!
You deserve tae be locked up, wi breid and watter behind bars,
and mind oan this, fur certain shair, we'll no be readin <u>your</u> memoirs.

No – I never should have spoken out, incognito I carried clout.
Remembrancer, Remembrancer, we ken yer game, we're shoutin out!
I got fired up, I blew my cover, like a foolish young Boy Scout.
Remembrancer, we'll aye mind you, ta-ta tae you and aa yer crew,
'cause noo we ken, we'll follow through, we're heidin aff tae pastures new!

Note: The Remembrancer is the only non-MP or civil servant with a seat in the
House of Lords and House of Commons. His job dates back to Henry VIII. He
has a budget of £5.3million, a staff bill of £500,000 – including a team of six
lawyers – and he represents bankers' interests at the heart of our democracy.

Newhaven

*for the children of Victoria Primary School, Newhaven,
and honouring Greta Thunberg*

Heel-kickin hame frae a lang day at school,
lowpin ow'r the cobbles, like a wee whirlpool,
I breenge, I breel, and the willie-gous squeal,
gandigowsters blaw like a carlin's reel!

Herrin fur tea, then I lay doon ma heid,
tak oot a book, and hae a bit read
aboot Newhaven, the toon whaur I bide,
the mercat, lichthoose, harbour, and tide;

the white horses ride, ma een are closin,
nod-nid-noddin, doverin, doverin,
the blue saut watter croonin, dronin,
I'm driftin, sweemin, showdin, floatin

in a dwam on braid waves o sleep,
boats drift by on the Firth sae deep.
I hear a lanely sang o whales like ghaists;
nets in the moonlicht wave like lace.

Newhaven, Newhaven, sing tae me,
ma hame, Newhaven, wi yer dancin sea!

Fishin floats glent and drift –
tirlin globes like planets in the lift;
an auld wumman bendin
ow'r the net-mendin:
ma great grand-mither –
her darg niver-endin;

bairns playin peevers, lauchin in the street,
but when they faa, skint knees mak them greet!
They're stackin fish boxes tae mak play-huts,
Och – the clarty guff o deid fish guts!

Newhaven, Newhaven, sing tae me,
ma hame, Newhaven, wi yer dancin sea!

The tide rides in, and the tide rides oot,
sails they blaw and ships they hoot,
I'm nod-nid-noddin, doverin, doverin,
driftin, sweemin, showdin, floatin;

I see a braw ship – leamin, glisterin,
The Great Michael! – gowd decks skinklin,
a war ship built frae the forests o Fife,
its guns wud mak ye feart fur yer life!

Newhaven, Newhaven, sing tae me,
ma hame, Newhaven, wi yer dancin sea!

The Great Michael sails me intae the dawn,
ma tired een appen on a Newhaven morn;
news o faimilies drooned in the sea,
news o muckle men wha cannae agree;

news o wars, far, far awaa,
ile slicks spreidin on the oceans ow'r aa –
I dinnae want war, I want war tae cease,
a brave new warld that's a haven o peace.

Newhaven, Newhaven, sing tae me,
ma hame, Newhaven, wi yer dancin sea!

Daurk the sky, and cauld the wund blaws
throu ma hert, like jaggit ice floes;
but I tak a bit paper, and I scrieve a note,
float it in a bottle, like a bonnie wee boat –

tae the warld a message: tak tent o the young,
mind on oor lives, and this sang we hae sung;
mak the warld a new haven – hear oor caa! –
a braw new haven fur ane and aa.

Note: *The Great Michael* was a carrack (a war ship) of the Royal Scottish
Navy, built by King James IV of Scotland from the oak forests of Fife. She
was too large to be built at any existing Scottish dockyard, so was built in
the new dock at Newhaven, and launched in 1512, the biggest and most
heavily armed ship in Europe at the time.

Til Ungdommen
by Nordahl Grieg

Kringsatt av fiender,
Gå inn i din tid!
Under en blodig storm –
Vi deg til strid!
Kanskje du spør i angst,
Udekket, åpen:
Hva skal jeg kjempe med?
Hva er mitt våpen?

Her er ditt vern mot vold,
Her er ditt sverd:
Troen på livet vart
Menneskets verd.
For all vår fremtids skyld,
Søk det og dyrk det,
Dø om du må – men:
Øk det og styrk det!

Stilt går granatenes
Glidende band.
Stans deres drift mot død
Stans dem med ånd!
Krig er forakt for liv.
Fred er å skape.
Kast dine krefter inn:
Døden skal tape!

Tae Youth
translatit frae the Norsk

Ringit bi daurkest faes
gang intae yer time!
Unner a bluidy storm
noo tak yer staun!
Aiblins ye ask in dreid
unkivert, appen:
Whit suld I fecht wi?
Whit is ma wappen?

Here's yer shield agin aa blaws,
here's yer claymore:
faith in this life we hae,
the warth o man.
Fur aa oor future's sake,
seek it, tak tent o it,
dee if ye maun,
but grow and sturken it.

Quate the grenades gang,
sleekit baunds.
Reest their breenge tae daith,
reest them wi yer saul!
War is a sneist tae life.
Peace is fur tae mak.
Cast in yer virr,
fur daith maun tyne!

Da synker våpnene	Then aa wappens faa
Maktesløs ned!	wi nae pooer.
Skaper vi menneskeverd	If we mak mankind mense
Skaper vi fred.	we will mak peace.
Den som med høyre arm	Thaim that wi their richt airm
Bærer en byrde,	bear a burden
Dyr og umistelig,	dear, sae dear,
Kan ikke myrde.	canna murther.
Dette er løftet vårt	This is oor leal hecht
Fra bror til bror:	ilk ane til aa:
Vi vil bli gode mot	guidness we will gie
Menskenes jord.	tae oor yird and its life.
Vi vil ta vare på	We will tent wi love –
Skjønnheten, varmen	its braws, its wairmth,
Som om vi bar et barn	like bearin a bairn
Varsomt på armen.	doucely on oor airm.

Note: Johan Nordahl Brun Grieg (1902 – 1943) was a Norwegian poet, novelist, dramatist, journalist and political activist, distantly related to the composer Edvard Grieg. He served in World War 11 as a war correspondent and was killed while on a bombing mission to Berlin. His poem *Til Ungdommen* was set to music by the Danish composer, Otto Mortensen, and has become a well known Norwegian anthem. This translation omits two verses of Grieg's full poem.

Mariner

*a libretto in verse – a contemporary re-telling of Coleridge's
epic poem, 'The Rime of the Ancient Mariner'*

SCENE 1: A WEDDING RECEPTION.

Wedding Guest
Welcome, friends, to our wedding feast,
we hope you're having a ball!
What a pleasure it is to be here
in this palatial Mediterranean hall.
So glad you all could make it
to our Marriage on the Med –
the kind of place you have to see
at least *once* before you're dead!
Joke!
Our couple's favourite get-away –
top of their weekend list,
and to share it on their special day
is a chance that can't be missed.
They've taken the plunge, signed the pledge.
On their behalf, I welcome you all –
prepare to toast the newly weds
the moment they enter the hall!

Chorus of Sommeliers
Champagne like rain! Rain like champagne!
Fresh fountain of the grape!
We're coming round to fill you up –
a pleasure you can't escape!
Champagne like rain! Rain like champagne!
Fresh fountain of the grape!

Wedding Guest
No expense spared, as you can see –
only the best will do.
Success reaps the glittering prize –
and that's surely what they're due!
It falls to me to do the honours –
for I am next of kin.
My wee brother's the ugly groom –

Second Guest
Aaw – you rotter – that's a sin!

Wedding Guest
Joke! It's me that's the brute,
he takes my teasing on the chin!

Chorus of Sommeliers
Champagne like rain! Rain like champagne!
Fresh fountain of the grape.
Fine Pinot Noir and Meunier,
oak hints of Chardonnay.
Let *joie de vivre* pop all your corks,
hip-hip, hip-hip hooray!

Wedding Guest
I won't say 'You'll huv hud yer tea.'
Now that *would* be a sin!
We've laid on a sumptuous spread,
fit for a queen and king.
Our happy couple travel wide –
they're aye up in the air.
To suit their cosmopolitan style
we're serving international fare.

Chorus of Chefs
Oh wait till you taste it,
the flavours that lace it,
you'll never have munched on the like!
Lau Lau parcels from sunlit Hawaii,
lucious Shawarma from downtown Dubai,
fried Mantou from far-off Shanghai –
your taste-buds will crave to give them a try!
Malaga Tang from Sichuan,
rainbow Sushi from Japan,
and delicious pakora –
Oh, don't you adora spicy pakora?
Did ever a venue provide such a menu?
Wait till you taste it,
the flavours that lace it,
a triumph of sensual delight!

Wedding Guest
So cast aside care on this day of days –
let hearts be birds on the wing!
Loosen your metaphorical stays –
feast and dance and sing!

The mariner, a young man from the African continent, appears among the guests.

Mariner
Ha! – that is surely all I crave
to cast aside my woe.
But it's hard, Mr Next-of-Kin,
when you come from the world I know.

Wedding Guest *(aside to Mariner)*
Sorry, but just who ARE you, Sir –
a gaberlunzie man?
Did you gate-crash your way in here?
Are you in the seating plan?

Mariner
I am an ancient Mariner.

Wedding Guest
Ancient? You don't fool me!
You've no white beard, nor skinny hand,
you're young as youth can be!

Mariner
It's true, I'm young, but ancient too,
my story – old as life –
I *have* to tell, so listen well –
to this tale I am midwife.

Wedding Guest
Presumptuous upstart! Leave now – go!
You've no right to be here.
This is a day to celebrate,
no place for threats and fear.
(turning to guests)
So, charge your glasses now, my dears,
ready for bride and groom!
Prepare to toast the braw couple,
chained together till doom!
Och – only joking! Forgive the slip
from one who's stayed unhitched!
It's clear to all who know these two
each other they'll enrich.

Chorus of Sommeliers
Champagne like rain! Rain like champagne!
Fresh fountain of the grape!
We're coming round to fill you up –
a pleasure you can't escape!

Wedding Guest *(to Mariner)*
What – still here? Thought I'd made it clear –
you *must* leave *now* – get out!
I mean it, Sir, you can't remain,
your manner, your clothes, it's black shame
you're bringing here – a stain,
so don't make me say it again.
I've already asked you –

Mariner
To leave, yes, I know,

Wedding Guest
So go!

Mariner
I can't.

Wedding Guest
How so?

Mariner
Not till you've heard my tale.

Sommelier and Chef Choruses sing
Here comes our bride, her train a sail –
a hundred yards of silk,
red as the petals of a rose,

her skin like buttermilk!
Her groom as fine, his hair like wheat
in summer fields of June.
So strike up, band, for the lovely pair,
trumpet, drum and bassoon!

The bride and groom enter.

Choruses
Now's the day, and now's the hour,
they've tied the knot, they feel the power
of the shining promise made,
a pledge that sheds for them a light
in darkest hours, a flame so bright
it leads them ever on
along the winding, unknown trail,
the joy and pain of life's travail,
in union they are strong!

Mariner
Sing your hearts out all day long,
I'll not leave till you hear *my* voice.

Wedding Guest *(aside to Mariner)*
It's neither time nor place!

Mariner *(grabbing Wedding Guest's arm)*
The moment's now – it's not my choice –
my words you must embrace!

Wedding Guest
Unhand me, man! I won't be touched
by one from who knows where –
you have no right to make demands –

unfix me with that stare!

Children sing as they appear through shadows like ghosts.

Children's Chorus
Nine fathoms deep we lie tonight,
far from the homes we know,
nine fathoms deep on the cold sea-bed,
our bodies drift like snow.

Wedding Guest
Mariner – tell me, who are they?
Their plaintive cry, strikes fear
into my soul! They seem so dead
and yet they move – are they really here?

Children's Chorus
Nine fathoms deep, we lie tonight,
far from the homes we know,
numb to the silken sharks and whales,
that brush us to and fro.
The ghostly moon above us sails
in a black and careless night,
for all their light, the stars are blind,
we're lost to humankind;
our dreams migrate like paper kites,
dissolve, fade, evaporate.

The children's chorus disappears.

Wedding Guest
Mariner – your glittering eye
turns my blood to ice, my mind to mist…

Mariner
I am an Ancient Mariner,
and you cannot resist,
no matter what you think of me,
the man from 'who knows where' –
I tell you this, for what it's worth,
we're all from somewhere else;
the world is wide and since its birth,
the changing tide of time has moved
all tribes through war and peace,
from over here to over there,
and back again, to who knows where,
and I am here, but I've been there,
and that is why my glittering eye
forever snares folk with a stare
that carries all those odysseys,
and a thousand terrors on the way,
and the penance, the debt we all must pay;
I may be young, but I am old,
I've been bought, and I've been sold;
and in spite of the joy we see unfold
here in your gorgeous hall of gold,
mine is the tale
that must,
this night,
be told.

SCENE 2: A BOAT ON THE OCEAN. BRIGHT DAY.

Mariner *(to audience)*
Our hearts that day were full of fear,
as our temple slipped from sight,
but hope rose with the dancing waves,

the sky was blue, the sun was bright –
so bright the sun at height of noon,
so light the lamp of night – the moon –
ice white the lamp of night.

The light fades from daylight to moonlight.

Refugee Chorus
Water, water everywhere,
with its black, midnight sheen.
Water, water everywhere,
but none to keep us clean.

First Child
This is not the moon I know,
the one I see from home
that lights my room in dark of night,
and not the great sea foam.
Oh Mr Mariner, Mariner Man,
please make this boat turn back,
Oh let it take me home!

Mariner
There's only one moon in the sky,
North, South, East and West,
and only one sun too, my friend,
so go to sleep, take some rest –
think yourself mighty blessed
to be here, safe from war.

Sister (of First Child)
Yes, go to sleep, little brother,
here – lie against my arm.

First Child
I don't want you – I want my mother,
she'll keep me safe from harm.
I want the moon, the one I know,
Oh, take me, take me home!

Sister
Mother's gone, little brother,
you have to stay with me.
We'll play a game to help us sleep.

First Child
I don't want to be counting sheep!

Second Child
A guessing game – let's try I spy!

Third Child
It's far too dark to see.

Sister
There's the night sky
and all its constellations –

Mariner
There are more of those
than all the nations
on this great, wide earth.

Sister
So – find the one for your time of birth!

Fourth Child
There's mine! Taurus – the big Bull!

Fifth Child
I can't see mine – the sky's too full
to work it out. I'm Capricorn.

Sixth Child
The goat! I see it! Look – there's one horn
and there's the other!

Seventh and Eighth Children
We're Gemini – the Heavenly Twins!

Ninth Child
And I'm Pisces – the one with fins!

Sister
And Leo? Hands up if you're a Lion?
No Leos here?

Tenth Child
I see Orion!
With his belt and sword –
the hunter of the sky –
he looks like a great Lord!

Children's Chorus
Under the stars we all were born,
Leo the Lion, and Capricorn,
Aries, Taurus and Aquarius
and the Archer – Sagittarius.
It makes you drowsy just to think
of every star, and how very far
from us they are, how very, very far.

Sister
Sleep now, sleep till break of day.
The ocean deep will carry you safe
to welcoming arms – a good place,
with all the time in the world to play.

The children sleep, and night turns to sunrise

SCENE 3: THE OCEAN. DAWN.

Adult Refugee Chorus
Water, water everywhere,
no horizon to be seen,
water, water everywhere
and nothing in between.

The children wake up.

First Adult Refugee
The wind is rising now, hold tight!
These waves could sweep us over!
All hands must grip with all their might –
here comes a giant roller!

Chorus of Children
Oh Mr Mariner, Mariner Man,
please make this boat turn back!
See the lightning split the sky!
Listen to the thunder crack!
Huge breakers strike the deck – thwack!
The sun it hides, the sky is black,
the sea it boils – oh, take us back,
turn round and take us home!

Mariner
No more can I turn tail on our track,
than melt the moon, unhinge the stars,
shoot Orion, or freeze Mars!

Chorus of Children
Turn the boat, turn it round,
Oh, don't let us be drowned!

Mariner
You all agreed to take this trip.

First Adult Refugee
You promised we'd be safe –

Mariner
Yes – but not on a cruise ship!

Second Adult Refugee *(who is bailing)*
It's a leaky sieve!
All that money we had to give
for THIS!

Mariner
I didn't know – I did my best –

Third Adult Refugee
For a fee, yes – it's no jest!

Wedding Guest *(heckling from the audience)*
I see your downfall, Mariner –
tempted by filthy lucre!

Mariner
Wedding Guest, how can you know
the root or shape of my future?

Wedding Guest
I can smell a rat, when it comes to cash –
you're stained by filthy lucre!

Mariner
Blood has spilled with your stocks and bonds,
I was only a hapless broker.
Oh, Wedding Guest, you think you're immune,
as you strut through life's market,
whistling along to a careless tune
making me your easy target;
you may choose to stand and gloat –
but we're all in the same leaky boat.

Second Adult Refugee
Nothing but a useless sieve!

Refugee Chorus
He's right – it is, it's just a sieve!

Mariner
Keep bailing if you want to live!
(to Wedding Guest)
They blamed me, they baited me, I think
they even hated me – but all I did
was make a bid to leave,
to cut our losses, escape the bosses,
who thieve and weave a lethal net of war
till all that's left for us to do is grieve.

The refugees beat out their mutinous terror.

Refugee Chorus
We're dead meat, and you're a cheat!
All *you* ever do is deceive!
A back-street sneak, yes, you're a cheat!

Mariner
Agreed – I took a fee to get us out,
but not enough to shout about,
not enough to guarantee
a future life that's fancy-free!
Oh – let me be! I don't need love –
love's dead for me,
love died with all my family,
took flight on burning wings,
plucked my heart and buried it,
and here I am, without a chart,
I don't care what becomes of me.
So beat your drums, rum-tum-tum!
My heart is dead, you don't scare me,
let the storm bring my destiny!

The albatross appears and the storm subsides.

Refugee Chorus
Is this a blessing, or a dream?
This lovely bird – her feathers gleam,
so calm her flight, her gentle might
has quelled the storm –
mercy in her graceful form.

First Child
I know you, bird, I know you well:
my mother! – war has cast a spell,
changed your shape, and now you've come
to rescue me – I'll fly with you
to the peaceful land of clouds above!

The albatross glides around the boat, gently touching the refugees.

Refugee Chorus
See how she strokes us with her wings!
And wraps us in a cloak of love,
see how the mist and clouds dissolve.
Her spirit sings, more gentle than a dove!

Sister
Her eye, it holds our mother's soul.
Let's say a prayer to give our thanks –
her presence makes us whole.

Adult Refugee
Mr Mariner, come – bow before
our saviour kind and fair.

*The ancient mariner kills the albatross, which flutters down
onto the deck.*

Refugee Chorus
Oh, Mariner, Mariner, foolish Man –
why did you kill the creature that we loved?
How *can* you be so blind to spill
such sacred blood?
She quelled the storm, she brought us calm,
she came to save us all from harm.

First Child and Sister
Our mother has been snatched from us again –
she has been murdered twice!

Wedding Guest
Oh, Mariner, now you'll surely pay the price –
your tale is one of terror and of shame,
a crime for which you'll take eternal blame –
you'd better pray that you won't pay
for this with many lives!

Mariner
Oh, Wedding Guest, my soul is tearing
with a thousand jagged knives!
My heart was numb, my heart was dead,
my heart was ice, and cold as lead –
war had hijacked every shred
of my humanity – till I killed that bird!
When she touched me with her wing,
I felt no love – just the sudden sting
of hate, no time to think – fate
stepped in with all its weight
to dictate the next step.
That one crazed act has taught me
what I've done – Oh, I've been bought,
and I've been sold – my heart burns
like molten gold – but love, through sacrifice,
has brought me back into the fold.

Refugee Chorus
Too late! Too late! You reprobate!
We will not tolerate such evil in our midst!
Forever you'll be burdened with the blame –
now wear the creature's feather round your neck

to mark your sorry shame.

They place a huge albatross feather around the mariner's neck.

SCENE 4: DAY. THE BOAT IS BECALMED.

Refugee Chorus
Silent lies the ocean, silent rests the sky,
no land, no ships, no creatures break
monotony on the eye.

Mariner
Day after day,
we lay there, stuck,
day after day,
nor breath nor motion,
as idle as a painted ship
upon a painted ocean.

Refugees Chorus
Water, water, everywhere,
and all the boards do shrink;
water, water everywhere,
and not a drop to drink.
All our tongues, through utter drought
are withered to the root,
it pains to swallow, breathe and speak –
as if we're choked with soot.

Sister
Look – a sail! A ship!
Help is here, it's drawing near!

Refugee Chorus
It comes between us and the sun,
it's sails like dungeon bars;
Oh, ship, we pray by all the stars,
you'll rescue us, or we're undone!

A ship with tattered, ghostly sails appears, carrying a man and a woman – a grotesque cabaret duo.

Death's Mate
I may be the Queen of Hearts
or maybe the Queen of Spades,
but mine is always a leading part
in the story of your days.

Death
She is my mate, Oh, what a fate!
Her power is great and true,
I deal the cards, she rolls the dice,
we're always ahead of you!

Death's mate leans over the side and offers a hand of fanned out playing cards to the refugee children.

Death's Mate
Come on children – want to play?
Choose a card – have your say
in the lottery of your life!
Jack or King, or maybe an Ace,
does the smile on my gorgeous face
make you shy? Go on – try!
Last chance to change your fate!

Death
Trust her, she will *never* lie –
she's not a spy – we're squeaky clean.
You can tell by my black tails and tie,
and her blood red dress with its silken sheen,
though, truth to tell, our skin's a little green!

Wedding Guest
Mariner – say, who are these two?
They somehow seem familiar...
is she a bride – is he her groom?
My mind they do bewilder.

Mariner
These two bring ill, I feel their chill,
I sense their dark intent –

Wedding Guest
Don't let the children touch those cards!
If so, their lives will turn to shards –
this pair mean to torment!

Death's Mate *(to children)*
You won't join in?
No matter – I will *always* win!
And look – I have! The game is done!
I've won! I've won!

Death
She's won!

Death's mate whistles three times, and they sail away.
Mist drifts onto the refugees' boat.

SCENE 5: THE REFUGEES ARE SLOWLY DYING AS THEY SING.

Refugee Chorus
We are lost. Are we the cost
of the world's other half? Tossed
on the waves of holocaust,
no nourishment – no food, no drink,
our bodies wither, till we shrink
to naught beneath the moon's rime-frost.

Chorus of Refugee Children
Nine fathoms deep, we'll lie tonight,
far from the homes we know,
numb to the silken sharks and whales,
that brush us to and fro.

Wedding Guest
Oh, tell me, Mariner,
tell me it isn't true!
Those people didn't die like this
nine fathoms deep in the cold abyss –
five-times-fifty women and men –
that little boy, and his sister too –
tell me it *can't* be true!

Mariner
Oh, Wedding Guest, why *would*
I mock the truth? This tale's so true
it burns right through, gnaws
like a tiger at my mind – the death toll
strikes at my very soul,
only me on the lonely waves,
bailing bodies instead of water –

five-times-fifty wasted lives
over the side – alone, just me,
alone on a wide, wide sea.

Chorus of Refugee Children
The ghostly moon above us sails
in a black and careless night,
for all their light, the stars are blind,
we're lost to humankind;
our dreams migrate like paper kites,
dissolve, fade, evaporate,
fade, migrate, evaporate...

Mariner
I tried to pray, but no words came,
I tried to pray, but my thoughts were lame –
a jangling babble – I couldn't claim
to know even my own name!

Wedding Guest
Mariner, Ancient Mariner man,
you never, ever should have slain
that mighty Albatross – I fear
this cross you'll always have to bear.

SCENE 6: ARRIVAL OF THE WATER SNAKES

Water Snakes Chorus
We are serpents of the deep,
we slide, we slip, we glide,
we slither hither, we slither thither,
we quiver with pleasure just to be alive –
our sleek skin a jewelled river,

like the shimmering veil of a bride.
We rise and fall, weave and coil
with ebb and flow of high and low
glittering ocean tide.

Mariner
Oh, blessèd vision of teeming life,
you pierce my heart with memory's pain,
your fellow creature I have slain –
the gentle Albatross – she came with love
to heal us all, but hate's gall blinded me.

Water Snakes Chorus
Northern Mangrove, Horn-Headed,
Beaked, or bright Yellow-Bellied,
we linger and mingle in spangled light,
and sometimes dangle in deep-sea tangle,
then come up for air on sea-shore shingle
till the breeze makes our skin tingle,
then we slip into the waves again.

Mariner
Bless you, and bless each living thing,
forever now your praise I'll sing
for the wonder to this world you bring.
Bless, oh, bless each living thing,
forever now your praise I'll sing.

The water snakes slip the feather from the mariner's neck.
The albatross rises again, holding the feather in her beak.

Wedding Guest
Mariner – it seems you are forgiven:
by blessing those creatures, you have driven

the curse of the Albatross from your life –
see her spirit rise!

The albatross glides away into the shadows with the water snakes.

Mariner
I cast my knife
there and then into the waves –
had I been wise
I'd have done so long before.

Wedding Guest
Ha! You mean, after the horse had bolted
you locked the stable door!

Mariner
I never will be truly free
From those five-times-fifty wasted lives
lost on this wide and lonely sea;
they trusted me, I took a fee,
and they paid dearly with their lives,
sisters, brothers, husbands, wives.
I took a fee, they trusted me,
their voices whisper on the wind –
never, never can I be free.

SCENE 7: THUNDER AND LIGHTNING. THE HERMIT APPEARS
ON A BOAT. HE IS DRUMMING WITH THE STORM.

Mariner *(calling out to the Hermit)*
Oh, Hermit of the Cedar Wood
of ancient times, your fame I do know well!
You are honest, true and good,

nourishing people with your spell
as you drum your tales by the fire
in your forest home. Take me from this hell
before the storm drags me down
nine fathoms deep!

Hermit *(drumming loudly and chanting)*
Greetings, Mr Mariner Man!
You look like you need some sleep!
What happened to your crew?
No matter – I'll do what I can for you:
by the spirit of our great mother bird –
killed, I'm told, by a careless hand,
I call on you, Elements – hear my word! –
in her blessèd name, the tempest I command:
slow down your beat, don't over-heat –
when I get going, you can't compete
with *me* for drumming up a mighty storm –
so, take a back seat, Mr Wind – *retreat*!

The hermit drums the storm into submission.

Hermit
See? He knows my word is very sweet –
Mr Wind don't need it spelled out twice!
No need for me to repeat, repeat!
All's calm now – coo-ool, nice…

The sails of the Mariner's ship crumple, as his ship sinks.

Wedding Guest
But look out, Mariner!
Your ship's breaking up,
going down like lead –

to lie a wreck
on the ocean bed!

Mariner
Never fear, Wedding Guest – I lived to tell the tale!
But I appreciate your kind care
in showing concern for my welfare!

Hermit
Swim to me! Quick – jump on deck!

The Mariner climbs on board the Hermit's boat.

Hermit
Well – that was a handy piece of luck,
just when you're about to come unstuck,
I sail by! You nearly were a dead duck!

Mariner
Blessings on you, Hermit friend!
I don't deserve to live.
Death befell my innocent crew –

Hermit
Yes – I heard they trusted you.
You took a fee, but didn't give
the care you'd pledged.
And that's your curse, Mariner Man –
from this day on, you'll have to dredge
your tale from memory's store to tongue –
this timeless song of exodus,
as sure as the heart-beat of my drum,
it always will be sung.
So, tell it true, and tell it good,

tell it in every neighbourhood,
through city, village, hill and dale,
let it ring out, clear as a bell;
and now, my friend – farewell, farewell!

The Hermit dissolves into the shadows.

SCENE 8: ARRIVAL OF MORE REFUGEES.

Mariner *(to Wedding Guest)*
That honest man delivered me to solid land.
And that's when I wandered through the town,
heard the sound of the wedding band,
and found my way to the bridal door.
I won't be the last, there are many more –
they may be dragging their weary way
right now, along a nearby shore.

Reprise of wedding music from first scene.

Mariner
The music calls you to the feast.

Wedding Guest
I've somehow lost my appetite,
to say the very least.
Mariner, I can't go back in there,
to chatter and pose for photographs – can't bear
the thought of all that
after what I've heard.
It would be absurd.

*A family approaches, exhausted, each parent carrying a child,
other children straggling behind.*

Mother and Father
Please help – we have nowhere to go!
Is there somewhere you may know –
a place with shelter, food and drink?

Mariner *(pointing to Wedding Guest)*
This man – he knows the perfect place!
Follow him!

Wedding Guest
Who – me?

Mariner
Yes – you!
In a blink he'll have you cared for –
plenty space!

More refugees appear.

Mariner
And here come more –
desperate people by the score.

Refugees
We were washed up on rocks and shore,
our spirits weak, our bodies sore –
from the roar of war we fled.
Please lead us to a welcome door.

Wedding Guest
(picking up a child, and giving another to the Mariner)
I'll lead you to that welcome door!
Follow me – I'll go before!

The Wedding Guest leads everyone back into the grand hall.

SCENE 9: THE WEDDING RECEPTION. TIME HAS
STOOD STILL. THE BRIDE AND GROOM ARE JUST
COMPLETING THEIR GRAND ENTRANCE.

Chorus of Sommeliers
Champagne like rain! Rain like champagne!
Fresh fountain of the grape!
Who's for another top-up?
A pleasure you can't escape!
Champagne like rain! Rain like champagne!
Fresh fountain of the grape!

Both Choruses
Now's the day, and now's the hour,
they've tied the knot, they feel the power
of the shining promise made.

Bride and Groom
Yes – now's the day, and now's the hour,
we've tied the knot, we feel the power
of the shining promise made –

Both Choruses
A pledge that sheds for them a light
in darkest hours, a flame so bright
it leads them ever on –

Bride and Groom
Along the winding, unknown trail,
the joy and pain of life's travail,
in union we are strong!

Both Choruses
In union they are strong!

Chorus of Sommeliers
Champagne like rain! Rain like champagne!
Fresh fountain of the grape.
We toast the bride and groom today!
Let *joie de vivre* pop all your corks,
hip-hip, hip-hip hooray!

Everyone toasts the bride and groom.

Wedding Guest
Dear friends, I hope you will accept
my apology for my absence here – time swept
me on its wing – I didn't mean to duck
my duty, but events struck:
someone came to intervene –

Second Guest
What do you mean?
No time has passed!

Wedding Guest
This man –

Third Guest
Which man?

Wedding Guest
My friend – the Mariner –

Second Guest
Where?

Wedding Guest *(pointing to the Mariner)*
Right there!

Third Guest
There's no-one – you're just stressed out –

Wedding Guest
This child in my arms –

Second Guest
What on earth are you talking about?!

Wedding Guest *(pointing to the refugees he's brought in)*
All these people! Are you blind?
There was a man, a ship, a crew,
they drowned –

Third Guest
It's happening somewhere all the time –
don't flay yourself with guilt!

Wedding Guest
But another boat-load made it through –
can't you see? They're as real as me and you!

Second Guest
Come – you've had a bad dream.

Chefs' Chorus *(mingling with trays of canapés)*
Food is served! Divine cream
of wild sea bream,
fennel and spice, with saffron rice!
Oh wait till you taste it,
the flavours that lace it,

you'll never have munched on the like!
Did ever a venue provide such a menu?
Wait till you taste it,
the flavours that lace it,
A triumph of sensual delight!

Wedding Guest *(to the refugees)*
Did you hear that, friends?
Eat and drink, feast your fill –
don't worry about who's paying the bill.

Mariner
No need – they can't see us –
perhaps they never will.

Everyone gathers and all sing:

There was a war, there was a man,
a ship, and a crew, they sailed a span
on the wide salt sea, and a bird flew
on wings of love, till she was slain.

Oh, may her spirit rise again!
Who will say who is to blame,
who carries shame, in this game
of win or lose?

It was told by an ancient bard
that there's a way, however hard,
to a place that welcomes all:
it lies far beyond beliefs
of wrong-doing and right-doing,
brighter than the coral reefs –
an open space, a shining field,

where hatred never is revealed.
Oh, will you meet us there,
and will you choose to live and share
the prayer of those whose only care
is to breathe the air of peace?

FINIS

Note: The final song includes a transcription of lines from a poem by Rumi, the 13th-century Persian Sunni Muslim poet, jurist, Islamic scholar, theologian and Sufi mystic:

'*Out beyond beliefs of wrong-doing*
And right-doing is a field –
I'll meet you there.'

Scots Glossary

aa – all
aawhaur – everywhere
ablow – below
aboot – about
abuin – above
ae – one
aff – off
afore – before
agin – against
aiblins – perhaps
aince – once
airm – arm
ahint – behind
airt(s) – place(s)/point on the
  compass
amang – among
an – and
anely – only
anither – another
appen – open
askit – asked
athoot – without
atween – between
auld – old
awa – away
aye – always/ever
banes – bones
ben/bi – by
bairns – children
beddit – bedded
bield – shelter
birks – birches
blin – blind
baured – barred
bide – stay/live

bluid-brainches
  – blood-branches
birl – whirl
blatter – loud, continual beating
blawin – blowing
bocht – bought
brae – a steep slope
braid – broad
braith/braithin – breath/
  breathing
brak – broke
braw – splendid
braws – beautiful things
breel – a whirring motion
breenge – rush forward
breid – bread
breists – breasts
brithers – brothers
buits – boots
caa – call
cairries – carries
cairts – carts
cam – came
canna(e) – can't
carlin's – witch's
cauld – cold
claith – cloth
clarty – filthy
climp – take hold of
cloods – clouds
coos – cows
cooshie-doos – pigeons
craigs – crags
cramasie – crimson
croon – crown

dae – do
daith – death
darg – a day's work
daurk – dark
davert – numb
dee – die
deid – dead
ding-dang – confusion, pell-mell
dinna/dinnae – don't
dirdum – noise, uproar
dochter – daughter
doon – down
douce(ly) – gentle, gently
doverin – dozing
dreel – a line/furrow
dreid – dread
drooned – drowned
drystane dykes – drystone walls
dule – grief
dunchin – bumping/nudging
dunder – loud reverberating
dunt/duntin(g) – thumping
dwaum/dwam – dream/
  daydream
een – eyes
eldritch – unearthly, frightful,
  hideous
faddoms – fathoms
faem – foam
faimily – family
faither – father
faulds – folds
faur's – far as
feart – afraid
fechts – fights
fidder – flutter
flichtert – fluttered
flooer – flower

fower – four
fowk – folk
frae – from
freends – friends
fremmit – foreign
fur – for
gairds – guards
gandigowsters – a sudden gust
  of wind
gane – gone
gang(in) – go/going
gantin – wanting something
  desperately
gean – wild cherry
gemm – game
gie – give
ghaist(ly) – ghost(ly)
glaikit – foolish
glent – glint
glisk – a moment
glisterin – glittering
gove – stare blankly
gowans – daisies
gowd – gold
greet – weep
gress – grass
growthie – fertile
grumly – grim
grun(d) – ground
grup – grip
guff – stink
guidness – goodness
hae – have
habbers – stammers
hale – whole
hame – home
happed/happit – wrapped
haud – hold

haurd – hard
hecht – vow
heeze – heave
heidin – heading
heiven's hicht – heaven's height
hert – heart
hirdit – herded
hornit – horned
howk – dig
hunner – hundred
hurdies – hips/buttocks
hus – has
ile – oil
ilk – every
insteid – instead
intae – into
lanely – lonely
larik – larch
licht – light
lig – lay
lowpin – leaping
jaggit – jagged
Januar – January
juist – just
ken – know
kythe – reveal
lang – long
lauch – laugh
leal – loyal
leamin – gleaming
lift – sky
links – sausages
lockdoon – lockdown
ma – my
mairlike – more likely
mair – more
mak – make
'mang – among

maskit – masked
maun – must
mercats – markets
merks – marks
messages – shopping (noun)
mey spink – primrose
mibbe – maybe
micht – might/may
mither – mother
moorit – reddish-brown colour
muckle – big
muin – moon
murther – murder
nae/naethin – no/nothing
naewhaur – nowhere
naw – no
neethur – neither
nicht – night
niv(v)er – never
noo – now
oor – our/hour
oot – out
ootthrough – throughout
owerseen – overseen
peedie (Orcadian) – little
peevers – the game of hopscotch
pirn-threid – cotton thread
pouer – power
prent – print
quate – quiet/calm
quine – woman/girl
raired – roared
reeshle – rustle
reest – halt, arrest
reid – red
reive – steal
richt – right
ringit – surrounded

sab – sob
sae – so
saft – soft
sair – sore
sairch – search
sangs – songs
sark – shift (a woman's garment)
saul – soul
sauld – sold
saut – salt
scraich – scream
scrieve – write
shairks – sharks
shairly – surely
shawed – showed
shooglin – shaking, wobbling
shoothers – shoulders
showdin – rocking/swaying
simmer – summer
skinklin – sparkling
skirlin – shrill, excited laughing
  (or screaming)
skraikit – screeched
slabhraidh (Gaelic) – the hook
  and chain for the pot over the
  fire
slaw – slow
sleekit – sly
smaa – small
smirr – a fine drizzle
snaw – snow
sneist – an insult, a sneer
snell – keen/sharp (of weather)
sodjer – soldier
soond – sound
souch – sigh
spreid(in) – spread(ing)
stairheid – top of a staircase

starns – stars
staun – stand
steek – shut tight
steekit – stuck
stooshie – turmoil
stour – dust
straik – stroke
strippit – stripped
strùpag (Gaelic) – a hot drink
  (literally, a small spout)
sturken – nurture
suddent – sudden
suld – should
sumph – oaf
swatshop – sweatshop
swaws – waves
sweem(in) – swim/swimming
syne – ago/then
tae – to
tak tent – take care
thae – those
thaim – them, those
the day – today
thir – these
thocht – thought
thon – that (place)
ticht – tight
til – to
tint – lost
tirlin – vibrating, quivering
toon's – town's
turnt – turned
twa – two
tyne – lose
unner – under
unkivert – uncovered
veesion – vision
virr – vigour, energy

waas – walls
wairmth – warmth
wappen – weapon
wappin – enormous
warker – worker
warld – world
warth – worth
watter – water
wecht – weight
weel – well
wha(e) – who
whae'd – who would
whan – when
wheemer – whine/complain
whiles – sometimes
whit – what
whaup – curlew
wi – with
willie-gous – seagulls
wull – will
wumman – woman
wund's – wind's
wunnerin – wondering
wuns awa – goes away
wyte – blame
yammerin(g) – wailing
ye're – you're
yez – you (plural)
yird – earth
yon – that
yowdendrift – snow driven
  by wind

Acknowledgements

SOME POEMS IN this collection have appeared in the following publications:

Staying Human (Bloodaxe Books, ed. Neil Astley); *Modern Poetry in Translation* (ed. Clare Pollard); *WRITE Where We Are Now* (online anthology, Manchester Metropolitan University, ed. Carol Ann Duffy); *Best Scottish Poems of 2020* (Scottish Poetry Library online, ed. Janette Ayachi); *Tell Me Good Things* (by James Runcie, Bloomsbury); *Hwaet!* (20 Years of Ledbury Poetry Festival, Bloodaxe Books, ed. Mark Fisher); *PENning* magazine; *The Herald*; *The National*; *The One O'Clock Gun*; *The Scores*; *Causeway/Cabhsair*; *Scots Hoose*; *The Leaves of the Years*, (Drunk Muse Press, ed. Hugh McMillan and Stuart Paterson); *Culture Matters* (ed. Mike Quille); *Scotia Nova* (Luath Press, ed. Alistair Findlay and Tessa Ransford).

Among these poems are included commissions by the Edinburgh International Book Festival; Alchemy Film and Moving Image Festival; BBC Radio 4; Scottish Poetry Library; YES Berwickshire; Glasgow School of Art Choir; Castle of Light, Edinburgh 2021.

With special thanks to Meg Bateman and Michel Byrne for their expert editorial assistance, and to Menna Elfyn and Dr Sylvia Warnecke for their encouragement; to my colleague the Gaelic singer Anne Martin, who, through Seall, commissioned *Song of the Slabhraidh* for her project *An Tinne*, 2022, Scotland's Year of Stories; and to my long-time collaborator, the composer Dee Isaacs, who, as leader of the University of Edinburgh's Music in the Community course, commissioned and composed our opera, *Mariner*, performed by her students and the pupils of Leith Walk Primary School, 2018, and also *Newhaven*, sung by her students and the children of Victoria Primary School, Newhaven, part of Scotland's Year of Coasts and Waters, 2020.

Luath Press Limited

committed to publishing well written books worth reading

LUATH PRESS takes its name from Robert Burns, whose little collie Luath (*Gael.*, swift or nimble) tripped up Jean Armour at a wedding and gave him the chance to speak to the woman who was to be his wife and the abiding love of his life. Burns called one of the 'Twa Dogs' Luath after Cuchullin's hunting dog in Ossian's *Fingal*. Luath Press was established in 1981 in the heart of Burns country, and is now based a few steps up the road from Burns' first lodgings on Edinburgh's Royal Mile. Luath offers you distinctive writing with a hint of unexpected pleasures.

Most bookshops in the UK, the US, Canada, Australia, New Zealand and parts of Europe, either carry our books in stock or can order them for you. To order direct from us, please send a £sterling cheque, postal order, international money order or your credit card details (number, address of cardholder and expiry date) to us at the address below. Please add post and packing as follows: UK – £1.00 per delivery address; overseas surface mail – £2.50 per delivery address; overseas airmail – £3.50 for the first book to each delivery address, plus £1.00 for each additional book by airmail to the same address. If your order is a gift, we will happily enclose your card or message at no extra charge.

Luath Press Limited
543/2 Castlehill
The Royal Mile
Edinburgh EH1 2ND
Scotland
Telephone: 0131 225 4326 (24 hours)
Email: sales@luath.co.uk
Website: www.luath.co.uk